Windsurfing

A DICTIONARY OF TERMS FOR THOSE WHO DO, THOSE WHO WANT TO, AND THOSE WHO WONDER WHAT ALL THE FUSS IS ABOUT.

WRITTEN AND ILLUSTRATED BY FRANK FOX

Amberco Press
Berkeley, California

Amberco Press
Berkeley, California

Amberco Press
2324 Prince Street
Berkeley, California 94705
10 9 8 7 6 5 4 3 2

ISBN 0−934965−03−X
Library of Congress Catalog Card Number 87−071488

Dedicated to all who have joined the eternal quest.

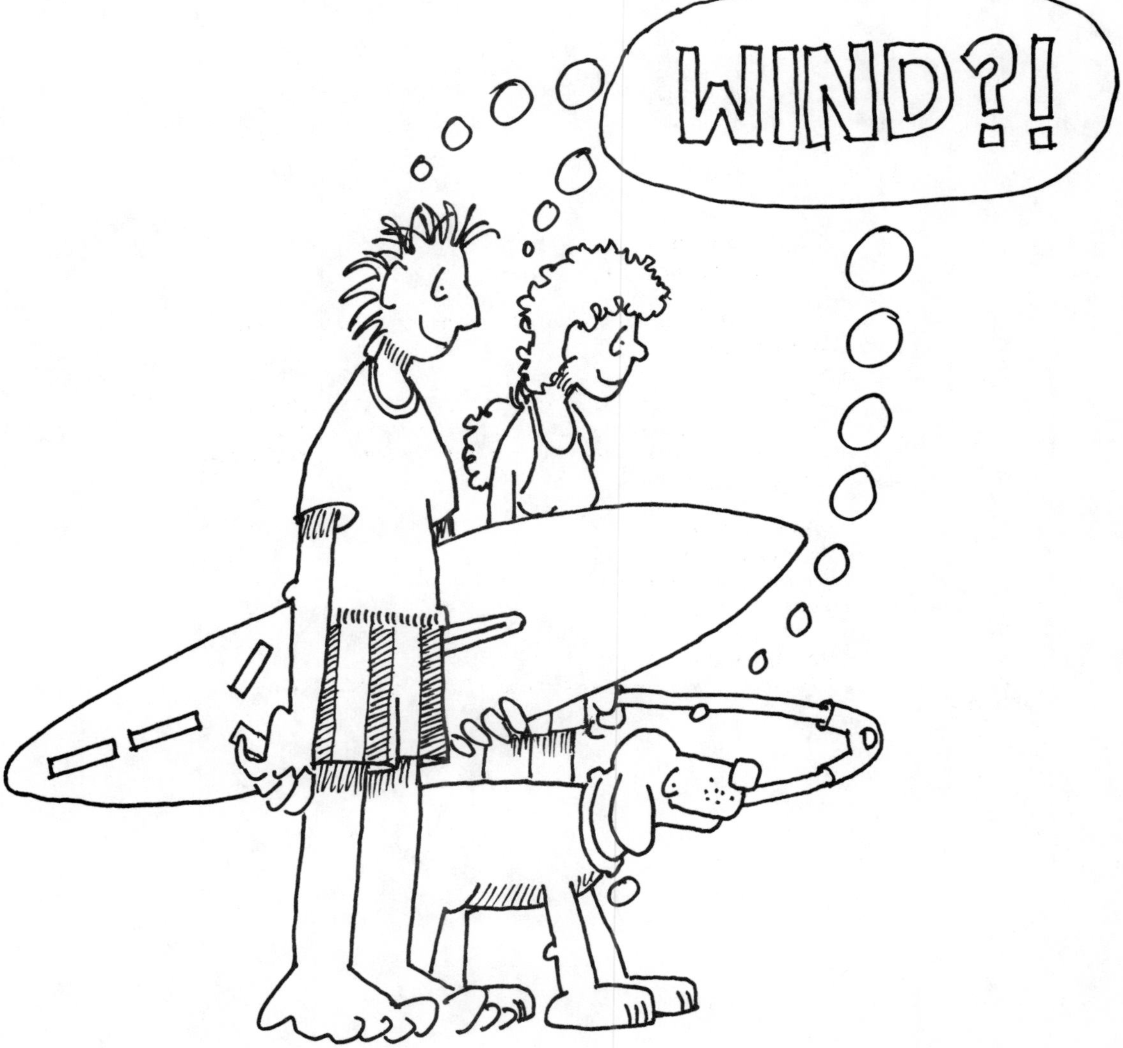

FOREWORD

Contagious Chuckles:

It's hot. It's the middle of summer, 1985. It's a minute before midnight. I have a press deadline tomorrow and I'm not ready. In front of me lays a large mound of notes waiting to be converted into news reports.

I'm beat. I goofed off and went sailing this afternoon. I stare at my pile of notes. From beneath, a funny little brown package ogles at me. It came with the day's mail. The package is vastly outweighed by the surrounding mounds of scrawl. It just lays there, unassuming, in no apparent rush to be opened. It has my full attention.

I open it. It's Frank Fox's *Zen and the Art of Windsurfing*. I leaf through. I chuckle. I laugh. I howl! I keep the old neighbor lady and her dogs up half the night.

She's old because she takes life too seriously. She doesn't windsurf. I'll send her a copy of the book, though I know she'll never understand.

Now it's the middle of summer, 1987 and along comes Frank with his second book, the *Windsurfing Dictionary* that puts into witty words what we've been trying to say for years. Unfortunately I've already lost my only copy. I write to Frank.

Dear Frank:

My stuffy old neighbor lady has moved out. My new neighbors are a congenial young couple. I taught them to windsurf. I thought they might enjoy reading your new *Windsurfing Dictionary* so I lent it to them. Now they make excuses when I ask for it back.

Then Mr. and Mrs Hummel, the elderly folks from accross the street, started taking windsurfing lessons from their kids. Yesterday, I watched Mrs. Hummel sneak a copy of the dictionary out of the house on her way to a waterstart lesson. I'm not normally suspicious, but it sure looked like my copy!

Wait! Hold everything! The neighbors down the street just drove by with new sailboards on their car. At this rate I'll never get my *Windsurfing Dictionary* back!

Please send another. Quick!

—Clay Feeter
    Publisher, *California Boardsailor*

A

Adjusting Screw

Any screw on a sailboard that, when not corroded permanently in place, can be turned, usually with the aid of vice-grips and a hammer, to set a release or control mechanism into one of two positions; 1) too tight, or 2) too loose.

Adrift

The cumulative result of being becalmed on an outgoing tide. The prudent boardsailor, in anticipation of such a distasteful possibility, will always carry a survival kit consisting of: 1) Three old copies of Playboy Magazine (with which to repay any fishermen who may come to his or her rescue), 2) A Spanish phrase book (in case he or she is eventually entrained in the Peruvian current), and 3) A VCR with the entire "Gilligan's Island" series on tape (an excellent source of prudent survival information which may also help to alleviate the boredom a boardsailor is likely to encounter during the months at sea).

Aerial

A difficult wave sailing maneuver performed by becoming air-borne from a wave face and then returning to the same wave face while, of course, maintaining control. Attempts at this maneuver have given rise to many more easily-perfected although physically more demanding maneuvers such as the *aerial face-plant*, the *aerial backslide* and the popular *aerial triple half-gainer with a twist*.

Aerodynamic Theory

A slang language popular in windsurfing circles which utilizes the grammar structure of Swahili, the verb conjugation of Chinese and the vocabulary of Greek. Although in existence and widely used in the scientific community since the early twentieth century, this language did not come into widespread use among the general windsurfing population until 1983 when gradually and for yet unknown reasons, aerodynamic terms began to appear in all but the most basic beach-side conversations. Phrases like, "It depends on the spanwise flow characteristics of the foil shape," gradually replaced "I'm not sure," and "Because of the laminar flow separation at the trailing edge," supplanted "Ask your father." For a number of years, Aerodynamic Theory provided windsurfers with a cult-like mystique since anyone outside the sport naturally assumed these people were speaking in tongue. This mystique continued until 1986 when a leading linguistic theorist presented a paper in which she postulated that, contrary to widespread assumption, the average windsurfer had a superficial or greater understanding of only 21.06 percent of a typical Aerodynamic Theory statement and only an 18.72 percent understanding of the answer he or she gave in response to the statement. In this light, windsurfers gained the image of unthinking creatures who simply mouthed current buzz words in order to give the appearance of expertise. This image, however, soon suffered an internal conflict which arose when many members of the windsurfing population, being bright enough to realize that such a reputation qualified them perfectly for a life in politics, decided to run for various public offices. Today, neither the "cult mystique" nor the "mindless creature" image prevails. Instead, windsurfers are simply seen as normal people who talk funny.

Aerodynamic Theory: The science of theoretical communication.

Bailing Out: Fully engaged.

Anemometer

A scientific instrument used for measuring windspeed which, through some quirk of modern technology, always seems to report a wind velocity only half that of the windspeed as simultaneously estimated by most boardsailors. Due to this fundamental inaccuracy, anemometers are not very popular in windsurfing circles.

Athwartships

A nautical phrase that, as it applies to windsurfing, means of, at, or relating to a position or positions perpendicular to an imaginary centerline struck on the deck or hull of the board. Often abbreviated as *like so*.

Athwhatships?

A typical boardsailor's response to a statement using *athwartships*.

B

Bailing Out

Also know as *constructive disengagement*, bailing out is a method of aborting a wave face maneuver which is widely recognized as the last and most decisive avenue of action open to a wave sailor who is otherwise entertaining the prospect of a trip to the emergency room. Although generally seen as life-prolonging, *bailing out* is not without its own trials and tribulations. One of the most important aspects of bailing out is properly dislodging one's feet from the footstraps before attempting to leave the board. A sailor who does not properly execute this small but crucial portion of the maneuver will no doubt discover new and exciting maneuvers such as the *shark bait body-drag*, *sucking up*, *thumping down* and, perhaps the all-time spectator favorite, the *cartwheel face-plant*.

Balance	A basic adult skill, the supreme mastery of which historically has been linked with early childhood and the use of a bicycle, but which is becoming increasingly linked to early insanity and the use of a sailboard. See *Inner Ear*.
Ballast (Increased)	A change in body mass which indicates that the number of calories burned by windsurfing for ten minutes does not necessarily justify the consumption of three beers, a hot dog, a pound of corn chips and two ice cream cones.
Batten Pocket	A fabric sleeve sewn onto the surface of a sail used to store sand, mud and small bits of kelp.
Beach Start	A method of starting the sailboard in ankle-deep water through which the boardsailor demonstrates his or her total disregard for the longevity of the fin.
Beat	1. To sail to windward. 2. To take out your boardsailing frustrations on your dog.
Becalmed	A state which, when attained farther than swimming distance from shore, has a tendency to turn agnostics into believers. See also: *Divine Intervention*.
Beer	An amber-colored, lightly-carbonated libation taken liberally during the ancient windsurfing ritual called "Restere per Ventare Grande" (alternately translated as "The Great Praying for Wind" and "The Praying

Ballast, increased (corn-chip induced).

for Great Wind") practiced religiously by devout windsurfers worldwide every Sunday.

Bite	What your dog does when he doesn't like being the object of your boardsailing frustration. See *Beat*.
BMF	Acronym used to describe a particularly large wave.
Body Drag	Originally, an inadvertent water-skiing maneuver which was adopted by the windsurfing community as a method of displaying total control of the sailboard. The link between total control and what appears to be a major underwater explosion, however, remains unclear to most observers.
Body Slam	An unintentional windsurfing maneuver named after the similar (albeit less painful) maneuver often observed in professional wrestling matches.
Booms	Four-dollar pieces of aluminum joined to six-dollar end-fittings with two-hundred-dollar rivets.
Bottom Turn	A sharp turn executed at the bottom of a wave which allows the wave sailor to sail back up the wave. From this position, the sailor can once again drop down the wave face repeating that exhilarating "I'm-about-to-die" sensation usually only attainable by falling through darkness toward certain death.
Bounce	A wave-sailing maneuver during which the sailor is rebounded off the ocean bottom after being thrust there by a large wave. According to practitioners of the maneuver, getting bounced is approximately equal in its entertainment value to a severe sunburn. Its advanced form, getting *dribbled*, should be avoided at all costs.

Breaker

A type of wave which tends to leave demolished windsurfing gear in its wake. Thanks to an internationally-accepted rating system developed recently in Southern California, these waves can be ranked in terms of their size and destructive potential into one of four categories: 1) Way Big, Man; 2) Like, Killer; 3) Totally Awesome; and 4) Mega-huge.

C

Catapult

(Origin, L. *catapultus projectile maximus*; to throw or hurl with great force as to maim or inflict great bodily harm). In 1969 windsurfing was invented. Fourteen seconds later the maneuver now known as the *catapult* was perfected. Bearing uncanny resemblance to a severe automobile accident, the catapult consists of hurling oneself nose-first toward the water at high speed and has become a mainstay of boardsailors worldwide. Recently, it has been suggested that catapulting itself become an Olympic event with scores awarded for both trajectory height and overall distance. Only survivors, of course, would be eligible for medals.

Caught Inside

A wave-sailing euphemism which, although similar in meter and cadence to "caught with your hand in the cookie jar" or "caught with your pants down," actually means to be smashed down on the ocean bottom by four-hundred-thousand cubic feet of falling water while hopelessly entangled in a flailing mass of

scrap aluminum and shredded fiberglass which, until four seconds ago, had been worth two-thousand dollars and represented your life's savings; certainly a fate far worse than the lack of pants or the presence of cookies could ever aspire to create.

Channeled Hull	1. A board with channels or shallow grooves in the bottom. 2. A board which houses the spirit of a 25,000 year-old surfer.
Charge Card Bill	A monthly statement of boardsailing expenses.
Chiropractor	A type of medical practitioner who caters primarily to avid boardsailors. Not to be confused with a *psychiatrist*, whose clientele is essentially the same but whose treatments are not physical in nature.
Clean Rounding	A buoy rounding during a race in which the boardsailor successfully knocks all competitors from their boards while maintaining his or her balance.
Close Out	The process by which a large wave asserts its territorial sovereignty.
Collision Course	Any course which, when maintained, can lead to catastrophic consequences. As such, windsurfers can be on collision course with other windsurfers, their credit card company, their mate or spouse, their boss or any combination thereof.
Coming Up	An oft-repeated weather observation based primarily on wishful thinking which is repeated almost continually with a chant-like cadence by beach-bound boardsailors.

Coming Up: A meteorological prediction based solely on wishful thinking.

Compaction Ratio	The percentage volume decrease a given amount of windsurfing gear undergoes during the process of shutting the car trunk.
Compressive Strength	The ability of a material to withstand the application of compressive loading as compared to that of empty beer cans.
Corrosion	How everything on a sailboard is held in place except that which is held in place by duct tape.
Course Evaluation	A set of calculations common within the nautical community, usually performed to determine if a vessel is on a collision course with another vessel. To evaluate your course: 1) Take an accurate relative bearing angle between your vessel and the other vessel; 2) Estimate the speeds of both vessels; 3) Plot your respective courses on the appropriate chart; 4) Mark a large skull and crossbones at the eventual point of impact; 5) Roll up and jettison the chart in a waterproof survival buoy; and 6) Turn toward the approaching vessel and, with your eyes wide in fright, scream at the top of your lungs the universal right-of-way hail "WATCH OUT YOU IDIOT!!" Since sailboards travel much faster than most other vessels, boardsailors find they are usually forced to skip steps #1 through #5 and begin with step #6.
Cut Away	A popular sail profile believed to relieve overpowering during gusts. Designed under the "less-is-more" philosophy, this sail is marketed accordingly, thereby allowing the boardsailor to pay an additional amount for sail cloth he or she no longer gets.

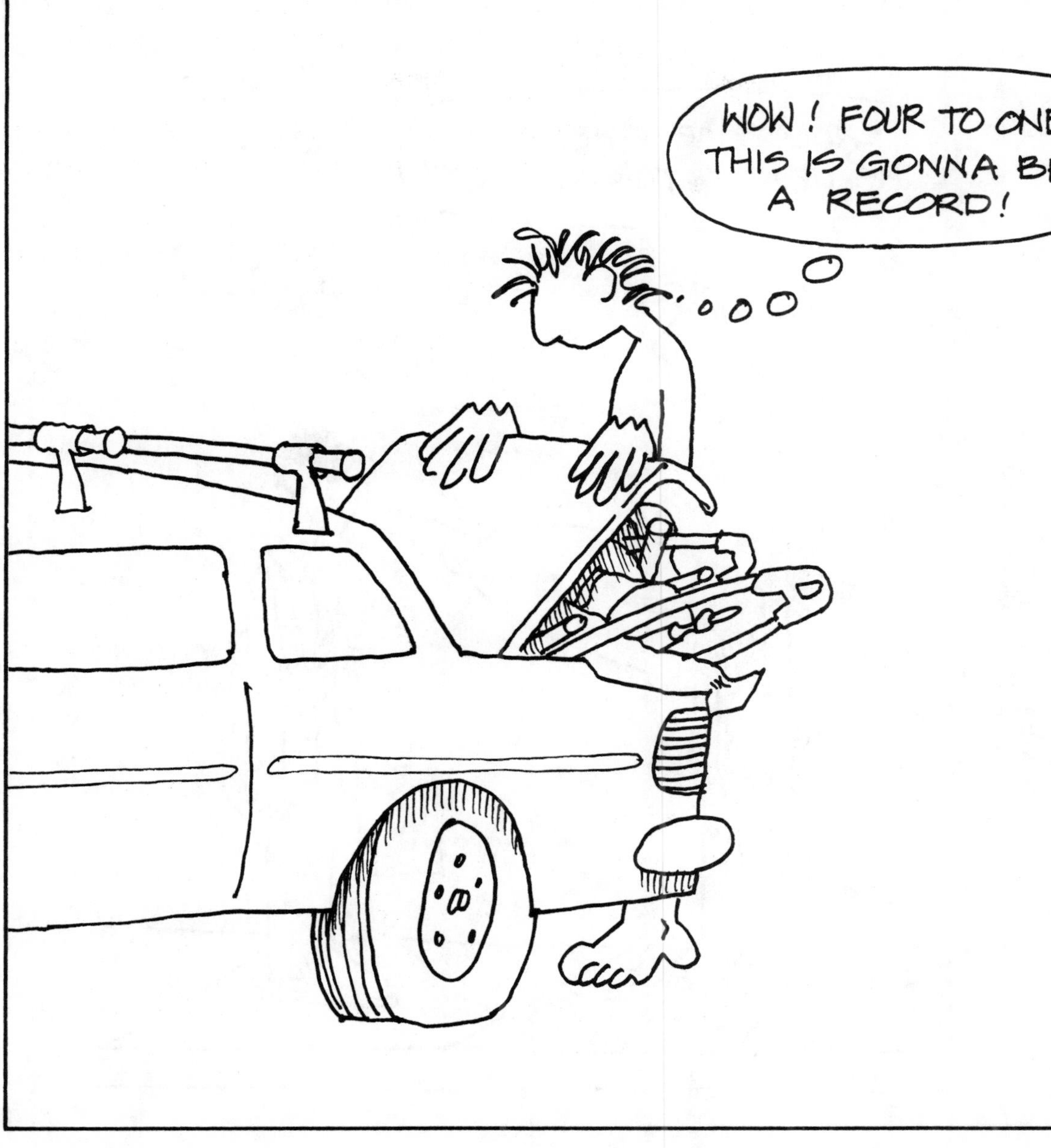

Compaction Ratio: Rising to the challenge.

Current: One of the hazards thereof.

Cutback

A maneuver performed as a last-ditch effort to control terminal *wrist rotation*. *Cutback*, or "cutting back" as it is sometimes called, is one of the most difficult of all windsurfing maneuvers. A few hints, however, might help: 1) Destroy all your credit cards, 2) Have your paycheck deposited directly into your spouse's bank account, and 3) Be more realistic about the resale markets for scrap aluminum and used mylar.

Current

Any naturally occurring movement of water which will deposit an object or person afloat in that water either: 1) At a shoreline of sharp rocks and broken glass, 2) In a vast expanse of knee-deep mud, or 3) To an area of the ocean from which the glow of the city lights can be seen over the horizon at night.

D

Daggerboard

A large, fin-shaped foil which extends through a slot on the deck of the board which ostensibly enhances the lateral resistance and improves the upwind performance of the sailboard. In actuality, it functions much better as a probe with which to locate sandbars, old tires and similar underwater debris. When such probing is not required, the daggerboard can be withdrawn from its slot and used for other things such as flailing at one's opponents during a race or, in a pinch, as a projectile to inform the race committee on how you feel about the general recall.

Dead Run

1. The point-of-sail achieved when the wind is directly at your back. 2. The speed at which most

boardsailors traverse the distance between the rigging area and the nearest pub at the end of the day.

Derigging	The time-honored art of releasing knots with a sharp knife or similar implement.
Destroy	1. Euphemistic description of what a good surf sailor can do to a wave. 2. Actual description of what a good wave can do to a surf sailor.
Distress	A gastrointestinal disorder developed when becalmed and drifting toward the shipping channels at dusk.
Distress Signal	A signal issued by any windsurfer who is faced with the prospect of spending more than twenty minutes without a cold beer. Usually distress signals vary both by season and locale. For instance, in New England during the winter, boardsailors issue the distress signal by allowing their body to turn stiff and blue. Conversely, during a Hawaiian summer, cartwheeling down a large wave face would be more appropriate. When in doubt, the prudent boardsailor should issue the *international distress signal* which is effected by floating face down in the water for a period greater than ninety seconds. If this fails to attract attention, the use of flares, hand grenades or similar incendiary devices may be necessary.
Divine Intervention	An oft sought and seldom received request for unworldly assistance for which certain future moral or ethical actions may be bartered. The significance of the actions offered in return for safety generally increases as the need for assistance becomes more acute.

Dock	Long, narrow, unstable, floating platform, usually covered with grease, algae, dead fish or similar impediments to untrammeled passage, over which novice boardsailors are forced to walk while carrying large amounts of bulky, heavy gear and enduring the scowls of anyone they bump, drip water on or otherwise deeply offend.
Dock Landing	A method of terminating a windsurfing session which often results in high-cost sailboard repair and substantial physical and psychological injury to those involved.
Dock Start	A freestyle maneuver similar to the *waterstart* except that the sailor begins sitting on the dock to windward of the board and ends up laying in the water to leeward of the board. While individual styles may vary, a properly executed dock start is generally seen to be one where at least five innocent bystanders are maimed and at least four hundred dollars worth of damage is done to the sailboarding equipment involved. Legislation to make dock starting illegal is pending in fourteen states. Feeling that most state legislators aren't adequately addressing the problem, the national organization M.A.D. (Mothers Against Dock starters) is also pushing for federal regulation of the maneuver.
Doppler Effect	Since sailboards travel at relatively high speeds, any sound emitted from the boardsailor is subject to the *Doppler effect*. Simply stated, this means that the sound waves traveling before the sailboard are compressed while sound waves following the sailboard are elongated. Hence, a boardsailor's voice is artificially high and shrill when he is traveling toward you

Dock Start (form correct).

and artificially low and elongated when he is traveling away from you. For instance, if you're standing on a pier and a boardsailor is approaching at high speed, what he is saying as approaching might sound like "IMGNA" whereas it might change to "DDIIEEEEEEEEeeeeeee....." as he passes beneath you and out the other side, if indeed, it doesn't stop altogether.

Dorsal Fin	A triangular-shaped object of dark legend the appearance of which, especially in large numbers, is generally seen as a bad omen by most boardsailors, especially if the boardsailors happen to be *becalmed* and/or *adrift*.
Draft	1. The origin or heritage of a pale-amber beverage popular with windsurfers. 2.(archaic) Term used to describe a sail's shape.
Drift	The speed at which you are going in a direction you don't want to go when boardsailing. Conversely, the speed at which you aren't going in the direction you do want to go. Some degree of drift is always present and can usually be categorized as: 1) acute (normal sailing conditions), 2) severe (heavy tidal influence), or 3) overwhelming (see *adrift*).
Drilled	A general description of the state a boardsailor achieves when impacting the water at high speed while twirling, tumbling, rolling or the like. Although getting drilled is a distinctly unpleasant experience, the prospective wave sailor may want to prepare for this inevitable eventuality by going to the local public pool and practicing swan dives from the highest div-

Dorsal Fin: Establishing who's the boss.

ON SECOND THOUGHT, MAYBE I'LL GO BOWLING...

ing platform while clinging to a fully-rigged board and sail. To make the maneuver more realistic, wait until the pool has been drained.

Dropping In	Unexpectedly visiting the bottom of a large wave face after which the dropee might unexpectedly visit the emergency room.
Drowned	A medical condition that occurs when novice board-sailors, due to the amount of time they spend in the water, actually begin to believe they are fish.
Drysuit	A piece of windsurfing apparel resembling a cross between a tuxedo and a body cast which acts to keep the boardsailor warm and dry. Designed according to the same principles used to develop the modern straight jacket, the donning and removal of the dry-suit usually takes a minimum of two participants and is considered by many leading exercise special-ists to provide an adequate daily aerobic workout for all parties involved. Although the difficulties associ-ated with getting into and out of a drysuit are far outweighed by the comfort they afford, their use is not recommended when sailing alone since they have been known to become stuck in the dreaded "half-off" position, causing the hapless wearer to drive to the nearest fire station for assistance with his or her vision restricted by the size of the drysuit wrist opening.
Dubious	The look that appears in most sane people's eyes when faced with the prospect of climbing aboard a sailboard for the first time. Often accompanied with phrases like: "You expect me to stand on *that*!!!??"; "Where's the steering wheel?"; "I think someone at-

Eating It: When a wave gets hungry.

tached the anchor to the sail!"; and "I want my money back!!"

Duck Jibe!	A warning issued to nearby boardsailors by a sailor who is about to attempt a jibe; very similar in intent to a golfer yelling "Fore!" prior to driving.
Duct Tape	A high-faith method of joining critical parts used in place of riveting, bolting, gluing, screwing and welding in most windsurfing systems.

E

Eating It	A wave sailing euphemism associated with being crushed by a large wave. The truth is, you don't eat it, it eats you. A more accurate expression might be *drinking it*, *swallowing most of it*, *drowning under it* or the like.
Ebb Tide	See: *Outgoing Tide*, *Becalmed*, *Adrift* and *Hopeless Situation*.
Electrolysis	1. An electrochemical process by which discrete metal pieces in the presence of salt water are broken down into their basic chemical constituents and then re-congealed into a single, amorphous rusty lump. 2. The reason you can never get your wetsuit zipper open.

Expenses, incidental (no bank financing required).

Expense, Incidental	Any expense directly related to windsurfing which totals less than a week's salary.
Expense, Major	Any expense directly related to windsurfing for which bank financing is required. Some examples of major expenses are upgrading to the current season's equipment, buying a new slalom board or paying for certain types of reconstructive dental surgery.
Extensions	Various lengths of aluminum tubing which enable you to make your booms either too long or too short.

F

Face Plant	(Origin, L. *faceus plantus*; to bury or furrow deeply and with great force). The instantaneous process by which the power harnessed in the sail is transferred to the surface of the water via the molecular excitation of the tissue of the forehead, nose, lips, cheeks and chin. Also called "Hoyle's revenge."
Fear Factor	A little-understood psychological process by which a subject's perception of things such as windspeed and wave height is drastically altered, usually by a factor of two or more.
Fiberglass	A modern super-material impervious to everything except bumping, banging, tapping, scraping, scratching, chafing, dropping, sunlight, roof racks and water.

Fin	A foil-shaped probe attached to the tail of the board used to locate rocks, sandbars and submerged debris.
Fin Box	A break-away device designed to protect the fin in case of collision with a submerged rock or similar object or from the normal bending stresses associated with everyday sailing.
First Weather Leg	The crucial first leg of a sailboard race during which racers attempt to gain tactical advantage over competitors while cautiously avoiding the violation of any state or federal handgun laws, the act of which may be grounds for disqualification.
Flotsam	Technically speaking, flotsam is floating trash (such as shredded fiberglass, gouged foam and tangled aluminum) which is unintentionally set afloat. This is as opposed to *jetsam* which is floating trash (such as shredded fiberglass, gouged foam and tangled aluminum) which is intentionally set afloat. In windsurfing, a fine and sometimes blurred line separates flotsam and jetsam. For instance, during a particularly disastrous wave face maneuver, your windsurfing gear may indeed become flotsam. If, at the end of the maneuver, you opt simply to save your life and don't attempt to salvage your gear, it then becomes jetsam.
Fog	Dark, grey, dismal visual obstruction often found on the lenses of one's glasses.
Footstrap	1. A small hoop of nylon or plastic placed in groups on the deck of a sailboard intended to prevent un-

First Weather Leg: Its effect on normally passive personalities.

Freestyle (advanced).

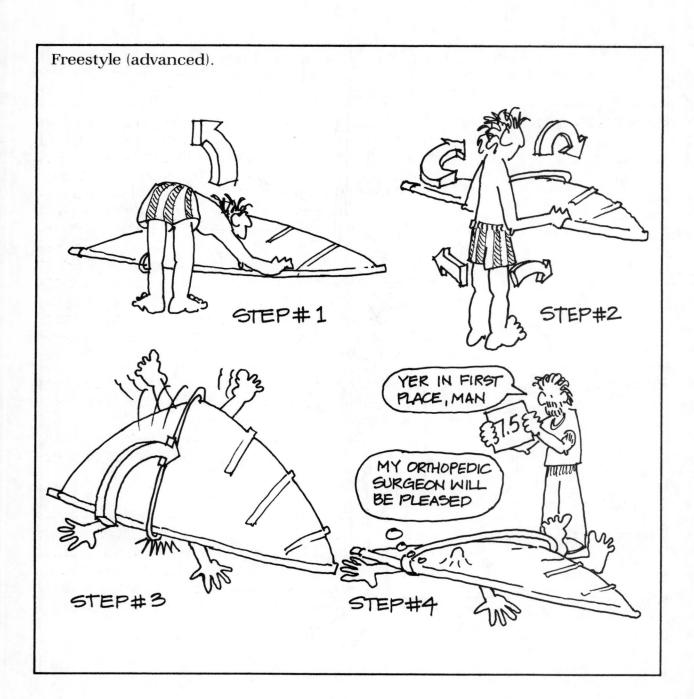

authorized use by making standing on the board impossible. 2. A luggage handle for a sailboard.

Foreshortening	A psychologically-based distortion in visual perception which, when on the water, causes the shore to appear much closer than it actually is. *Foreshortening* is common among boardsailors with intact gear and in times of abundant wind. If the wind dies unexpectedly or a piece of crucial gear fails, the reverse distortion, "Swimmer's Syndrome," usually occurs. Here the shore appears even more distant and remote than it really is. An advanced form of this latter condition is called "Fin Syndrome" and is brought on by the appearance of a large dorsal fin. This syndrome causes the shore to appear incredibly distant even though there is abundant wind and the possibility of gear failure is remote.
Freestyle	A type of windsurfing competition which combines the disciplines of log-rolling, break dancing and gymnastics during which competitors perform a practiced routine and are judged according to the basic physical impossibility of the maneuvers they perform.
Freighter	See *Tonnage Rule*.
Frozen	An advanced stage of hypothermia characterized by slurred speech and loss of motor control. As such, it usually requires an expert medical opinion to determine if the apparent victim is actually suffering from hypothermia or is simply recovering from last night's regatta party.

G

Gearbag
A large canvas or nylon zippered sack used by boardsailors to store and transport miscellaneous gear. Extreme care must be taken in the use of a gearbag since the presence of discrete aluminum pieces, petrochemical plastics and salt water in a dark, sealed space such as the interior of the gearbag provides both the electrolytic activity and the petri dish environment that, when heated to the approximate temperature of a car trunk on a sunny summer day, is seen by many leading biologists as providing the necessary ingredients to create life, or at least instantly propagate any lowly forms which may already be present. Should you find your gearbag bloated, oozing a greenish-brown organic paste, and/or smelling like Godzilla's tennis shoes, it would be best to dispose of it by incineration. Hand grenades, although used with limited success through 1982, sometimes simply release a mutated form of the organism to the environment.

Geek
In theory, a novice boardsailor that doesn't know what he or she is doing. In practice, how everyone who windsurfs refers to anyone else who windsurfs that they don't personally know.

General Recall
The restart of a race called for when, in the opinion of the race committee, not enough contestants were maimed in the original starting procedure.

God-in-a-Box
See *Weather Radio*.

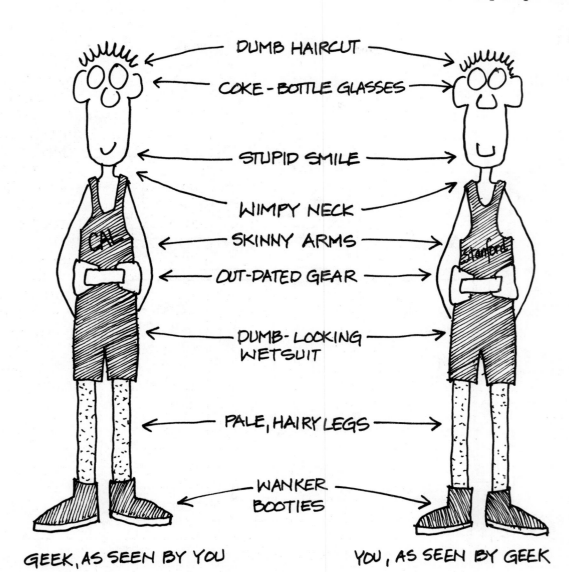

Geeks (in perspective).

Head Dip: Proper termination of the maneuver.

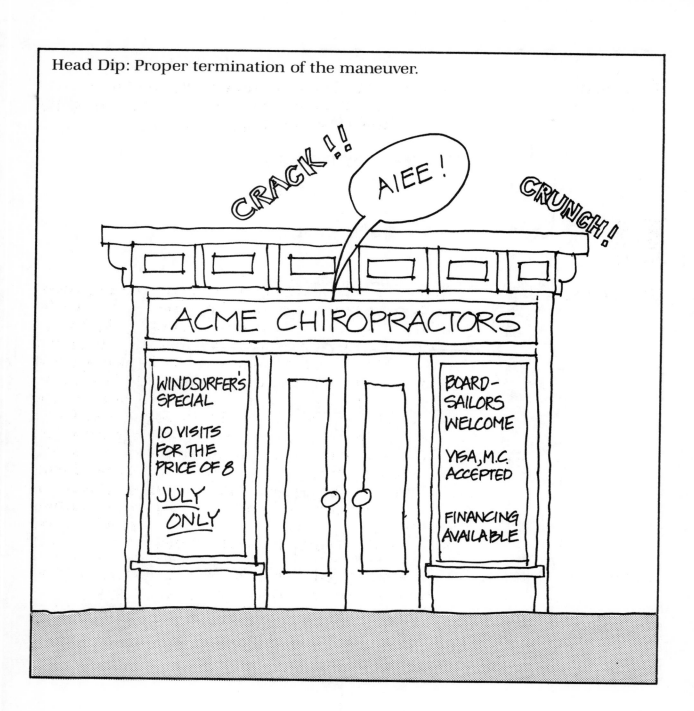

Good Start	Any race start, no matter how badly the racing rules are violated, during which you manage to attain the most advantageous starting position.

H

Hail/Counter Hail	A hail is something said to an approaching vessel usually to indicate that the hailer intends to exercise a right-of-way over the hailee. A counter hail is an answer to a hail. The most common hails used are "Starboard!" (a boat on starboard tack has right-of-way over a boat on port tack); "Leeward!" (a leeward boat has right of way over a windward boat on the same tack); "Sea room!" (indicating that the hailer feels he or she is being forced into unnavigable water by the hailee); and "Uninsured!" (indicating that the hailer is currently sailing the sum of his or her financial assets, the remains of which might be all you can collect in case of a collision). The respective counter hails to these hails are, "What?"; "Huh?"; "Say again?"; and "Please go ahead, I'll tack."
Hawaii	A mythical land of warm, steady winds where good boardsailors go when they die.
Head Dip	A freestyle maneuver during which, while sailing along, the boardsailor bends over backwards and re-

peatedly bounces his or her head in and out of the water. First introduced in 1971 by the ISUC (International Society of Underemployed Chiropractors), the head dip is now encouraged by physical therapists everywhere.

High Tide	1. A rise in the ocean level caused by the interacting gravitational pulls of the earth and moon. 2. The reason your board is no longer down on the beach where you left it.
Hopeless Optimism	A psychological disorder common among windsurfers which results from the long term belief in mythical or impossible things such as steady, abundant wind, warm water and inexpensive windsurfing gear. One of the most common manifestations of this disorder is a perceptual distortion which causes the boardsailor to be thoroughly convinced that perfectly still air is actually in the process of becoming perfectly sailable wind. See also: *Coming Up*.
Hopeless Situation	Any circumstance over which a participant has little or no control. Some of the more common *hopeless situations* one finds in windsurfing are *uphauling, dock starting, tacking, jibing, pointing, reaching, running, drifting* and *signaling for help*.
Hydrodynamic Theory	A slang language similar to Pig-Latin commonly used among windsurfers to confuse anyone who might be eavesdropping. See also: *Aerodynamic Theory*.

Learning to Jibe: The fine art of deliberated thought.

STEP #1: ATTEMPT TO JIBE. CAREFULLY ANALYZE ANY PROBLEMS YOU ENCOUNTER.

STEP #2: WORK TOWARD A SWIFT & PERMANENT RESOLUTION OF THOSE PROBLEMS

I

Inconsistent
1. Description of irregular surf conditions or wave sets. 2. Description of an avid windsurfer's summer-time employment attendance record.

Induced Wind
Air movement that is driven by something other than atmospheric conditions. Most commonly, the thermally driven upward movement of air readily observed when boardsailors gather to recount the day's harrowing tales.

Inner Ear
The human body's natural balance mechanism which, empirical evidence suggests, ceases to function properly when the soles of a subject's feet come into contact with epoxy, polyester, PVC, ABS or any similar material from which sailboards are manufactured.

J

Jellyfish
A primitive aquatic invertebrate resembling a small plastic bag and capable of inspiring as much fear in a boardsailor as a shark.

Jibe
A fundamentally impossible method of turning a sailboard designed primarily to entertain spectators.

Learning Experience: A type of avoidance conditioning.

K

Knot

1. An abbreviation for "nautical mile-per-hour" that defies all but phonetic logic. 2. Any one of various technical methods used for securing two pieces of rope or line such that releasing them doesn't require the use of a hydraulic ram, prudently-placed plastic explosives or razor-like device.

L

Landing

The second and most crucial step in a jump maneuver. Also the most difficult and the most likely to induce acute physical, psychological and financial stress if performed incorrectly.

Learning Experience

Any catastrophic and generally inadvertent maneuver which leaves the boardsailor sufficiently shaken to discourage future attempts at repetition. See: *Catapult*, *Face Plant*, and *Dock Start*.

Le Mans Start

A type of race start where competitors line up on the beach and, when given the signal, sprint down the beach to grab their gear and continue to the water. Named after the infamous 12th century French barbarian Jean-Paul "Le Terrible" Le Mans, this type of race start attempts to resurrect the lost martial arts

Masochist: A night at "Masochists Anonymous."

of jousting, clubbing, spearing, stabbing and running over one's helpless opponent.

Load Capacity	The amount of structural stress on any piece of windsurfing gear that, when exceeded, can lead to acute financial stress.
Loading	The process of fitting eighty-six cubic feet of windsurfing paraphernalia into eighteen cubic feet of automobile trunk space. See also: *Compaction Ratio*.

M

Masochist	A societal deviant who takes pleasure in various forms of pain. For instance, a masochist might enjoy dressing up in skin-tight black rubber while being repeatedly dipped in ice-cold water, knocked and poked with miscellaneous aluminum tubing and worked until physically exhausted.
Mass Confusion	A general state of disarray attainable at its highest level only during the last fifteen seconds of a sailboard race starting sequence.
Mast	A long, thin, cylindrical piece of aluminum or fiberglass tapered at one end and engineered to produce catastrophic failure at the worst possible moment.
Mast Base	An adjustable mast extender which, when used within 20 miles of salt water or beach sand, becomes solidly and permanently stuck in one position. Al-

Mast Base Adjusting Pin: Losing it for the last time.

though initially viewed with some irritation by most boardsailors, this tendency of the mast base to solidly jam in position is eventually welcomed since the crucial mast base adjusting pin is approximately 2 microns long by .05 microns in diameter and tends to be permanently absorbed when dropped on grass, sand, gravel, carpet, upholstery, asphalt, tile, metal, weeds, concrete, dirt, terrazzo, wood or other similar surfaces.

Mast Base Adjusting Pin

In 1984, while attempting to develop a high-strength mechanical fastener for use on printed circuit boards, Dr. Vladamir Rubinoffski produced an incredibly small, super-strong metal pin which was later adapted for use as an adjusting pin in adjustable mast base systems. Unfortunately, due to its size, the adaptation of this pin for this particular use gave rise to a tremendous technical problem of accidental loss which has never been fully overcome. Responding to criticisms along these lines, in 1986, Dr. Rubinoffski presented the theory that, instead of being lost, when confined to gear bags, glove compartments and similar areas, the adjusting pin actually mutates into a life-form closely resembling old candy bar wrappers and beach sand. Although the empirical evidence to support such a theory is overwhelming, Dr. Rubinoffski has never been able to duplicate these results in the laboratory environment.

Mast Foot

1. A medical condition common to novice windsurfers which develops when allowing the mast to fall forward before getting the forward foot behind the

mast step. Generally marked by the extensive use of colorful slang at high volumes, the telltale symptom of this condition is four or more broken toes on one foot. 2. An increment of length or stature given by the square root of your mast length in board widths.

Mast High A measure of wave height also referred to as *huge*, *awesome*, *incredible*, *killer*, *wow*, *(gulp)* and *jeez!*

Mast Track A long, narrow furrow on the deck of the board designed to catch sand and filled with usually immobile pieces of metal.

Mud Flats Areas of naturally occurring mud deposits, filled with old tires and broken glass and, for as yet unexplained reasons, often the chosen site for windsurfing schools.

N

Natural A person who quickly excels at a sport due to certain physical or psychological qualities he or she possesses. For instance, a natural football player might be one who has great sprinting ability, excellent peripheral vision and the intuition to sense how a play will develop. Recent sports psychology studies indicate that a natural windsurfer is a person who has the ability to: 1) Smile broadly while in great pain, 2) Smile broadly while totally exhausted and 3) Smile broadly while spending next month's rent money on the latest fin.

Navigation	As practiced by windsurfers, the fine art of finding your way back to your cooler on a crowded beach.
Nose	The bodily point of contact during a properly-executed face plant.
Nosing In	One of various unsuccessful and generally distained methods of landing a sailboard after a jump which can put you on a first name basis with your plastic surgeon.

O

Offshore	A wind direction, the normal presence of which usually indicates that a prospective boardsailor's longevity may be considerably enhanced by taking up another sport.
One-Handed Jibe	An advanced type of high-speed jibe during which one hand is used to jibe the boom while the other hand is used to protect the face and head.
Outgoing Tide	Any tidal flow which has the potential of introducing the boardsailor to the sport of *open-ocean drifting*. Fortunately, boardsailors who might find themselves entrained in such a tidal flow can reasonably expect the naturally-occurring repetition of tides to eventually deposit them at the point of origin, usually at the end of a 31-day tidal cycle.

Overpowered   A high-wind style of boardsailing which is most easily recognized by the elongation of the boardsailor's arms by two inches.

Over-the-Falls   A near-death experience that occurs between getting *sucked-up* and getting *pounded*, the cessation of which usually requires *divine intervention*.

P

Personal Flotation Device   A piece of safety gear (generally a piece of buoyant foam with a covering), required by law in some states, intended to keep the boardsailor afloat until help arrives in case his or her board (generally a piece of buoyant foam with a covering) sinks.

Plowing In   To make or carve a furrow in the water with your nose, especially at high speed.

Pocket Knife   A highly useful tool which, along with a rock, a rusty screwdriver, some duct tape and a can of WD-40, composes every windsurfer's major emergency repair kit.

Pointing   1. One of three basic points-of-sail which, when maintained for longer than thirty seconds, substantially decreases the possibility that the boardsailor will eventually return to his or her point of departure unless first aided by a motorboat or similarly

powered vessel. 2. A bodily gesture often used by a boardsailor to call attention to another boardsailor's ridiculous mistakes which, when combined with roaring laughter or similar unrestrained indicators of humorous entertainment within earshot of that other boardsailor, may lead to the acute need for dental repair.

Points System	A rating system used by judges to assess competitors' skills in surf sailing competition. Although the type of points system used varies from area to area, the "ten-point must system" is the most prevalent. Under this system, the sailor is assigned points according to the severity and number of bodily blows incurred while attempting various maneuvers.
Pounded	The process of fully absorbing a total wave experience.
Premise	A theory or idea which, although possibly unfounded, provides guidance and direction. Some typical windsurfing premises are, 1) If I don't buy it now, it'll only go up in price; 2) If I don't buy it now, think of all the fun I'll miss; and 3) I'm sure the bank won't care if I exceed my credit limit by a few hundred dollars.
Pre-season Training	A springtime exercise regimen used by avid boardsailors to prepare themselves for the coming season. Common exercises include ice-water immersion, self-flagellation and the all-important charge card curls.

Q

Quick Release   Any release mechanism found on a sailboard which is quickly rendered permanently inoperable by salt, sand, wind, rust or use.

R

Race   A nautical version of a demolition derby through which boardsailors can test their own ability to withstand pain and repair broken gear against that of others.

Racing Rules   A set of regulations used to govern competitive windsurfing events. It is recommended that the novice racer have a basic understanding of these rules prior to his or her first competition. Since the rules are quite lengthy and legally complex, he or she might want to study first an abbreviated interpretive manual such as *An Overview of Basic Racing Rules*, a ten-volume compendium published as a basic text with an eye toward simplified language. In a more practical vein, the 350-page manual, *500 Yacht Racing Rules, Fully Conjugated*, provides a summary of the most common hailing and counter-hailing sequences associated with various racing situations. For those interested in a deeper and fuller understanding of the racing rules, several major universi-

Quick Release: The occasional need for gentle persuasion.

ties offer a Doctorate in the theory and practice of sailboard racing rules under which the disciplines of Medieval Cannon Law, Personal Injury Litigation, Public Debate, Gunboat Diplomacy and Full-Contact Karate are combined to provide the student with all the basic skills needed to successfully compete in sailboard competitions.

Rating	A system used by windsurfing magazines to rank the respective attributes of different companies' boards and rigs. A four-star rating (****) means excellent. A three-star rating (***) means good. A two-star rating (**) means poor and a one-star rating (*) means that the company's advertising check bounced last month. A similar system is used by local board shops to rate their most frequent customers.
Reality	That which is avoided at all costs by avid boardsailors, especially during the summer.
Reef	A natural and beautiful underwater rock formation with surface characteristics somewhere between those of broken beer bottles and barbed wire whose proximity to the water's surface is usually of concern to surf sailors.
Reef Rash	An epidermal condition common to surf sailors who miscalculated the reef's proximity to the water's surface.
Regatta Dinner	A post-race meal, usually consisting of unidentifiable gruel, lumpy gravy and lime jello which is used as a justification for the forty-five dollar regatta entry fee.

Release Button	A button that, when used in conjunction with a sledge hammer, trips a mechanism, usually permanently, releasing the mast base from the board.
Rental Board	Any sailboard condemned by the U.S. Coast Guard or similar authority due to an inability to float or any similar condition that renders the board grossly unsafe or incapable of being sailed.
Repairs, Minor	The type of repairs a boardsailor can perform on a board or rig in the parking lot or rigging area using only a rock, an old tree branch, duct tape and a rusty pair of pliers that won't open.
Repairs, Major	The type of repairs a boardsailor can perform if he or she can get the pliers open.
Responsive	A board whose ability to turn exceeds the boardsailor's ability to turn it.
Ricochet	Any one of many maneuvers that results from the miscalculation of one's distance or closing speed to an obstruction.
Rigging	A curious pre-sailing ritual in which, after expending considerable time and mental energy carefully weighing all possible options and all available data, the boardsailor chooses and prepares a sail which is either too small or too large for the conditions.
Rigging Frenzy	A massive and concerted group rigging effort which is similar in appearance to a major riot or large scale civil disobedience and which is usually incited by the observation of an overturning leaf, a minutely-swaying tree limb or some other indicator which, when combined with unrestrained wishful thinking,

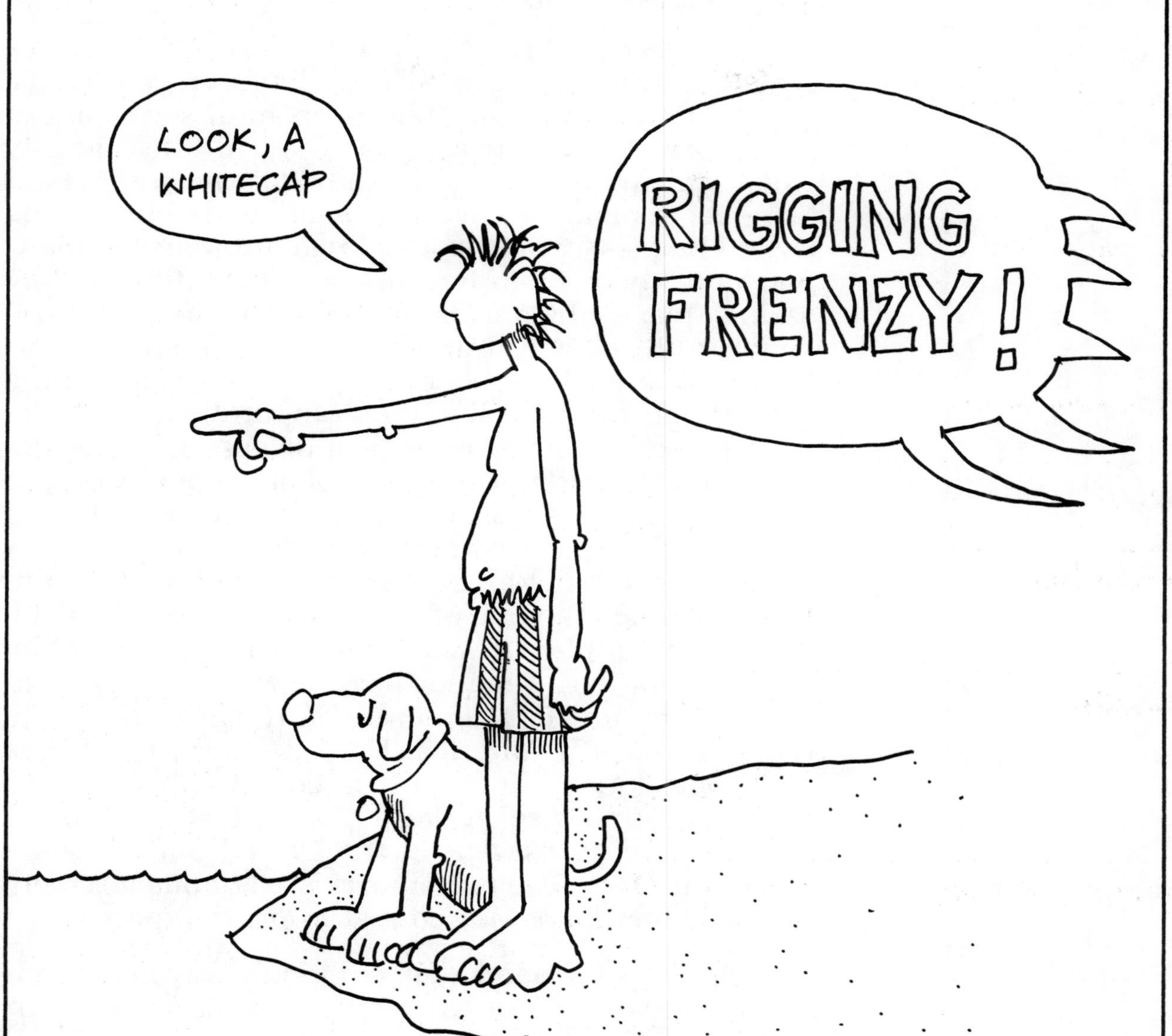

Rigging Frenzy: Innocently inciting a riot.

signals that the wind may be building from dead calm to three knots.

Riptide	1. A powerful current caused by receding waves which can sweep an unwitting victim far out to sea. See *Adrift*. 2. A popular television mini-series about three private detectives, played by Eddie "Beverly Hills" Murphy, Sylvester "Rambo" Stallone and Arnold "The Terminator" Schwarzenegger, who, while being pulled helplessly out to sea clinging to one sailboard between them, happen upon a beautiful young widow, played by Vanna White, adrift in a life raft, suffering from a terminal brain tumor and relentlessly pursued by mob members intent on gaining control of her family's oil company/winery/hotel conglomerate. During episode fourteen, Sylvester decides that Arnold's accent is probably communist so he pulls out a crossbow and shoots Arnold with twenty-six armor-piercing hunting arrows. This really makes Arnold mad so he chases Sylvester into the stamping machine of a nearby ocean-going metal reprocessing plant. Meanwhile, Vanna and Eddie convince Vanna's no-good brother's evil attorney to sell the family conglomerate and wire them the money in South America. Unfortunately, the funds are mysteriously diverted to a covert CIA cause. In the end, Vanna receives faith healing by Oral Roberts and becomes president of the United States, Eddie wins four Oscars, Arnold marries a famous celebrity and Sylvester buys Mexico just to prove he can.
Risqué	Description of a particularly difficult wave face maneuver performed on a particularly large wave in France.

Rock	A sedentary aquatic animal with an impervious and usually sharp outer shell which lives in shallow water and feeds primarily on fiberglass fins, mylar sails and the soft underbelly of human feet.
Roof Rack	Specialty luggage carriers used by boardsailors to transport gear atop their cars. Although specific systems vary, roof racks are usually attached to the car with high-strength structural rust, epoxy-modified road glop or a combination thereof. Roof-rack removal, once the realm of any competent mechanic with access to a cutting torch and a sledge hammer, is now a federally regulated profession requiring extensive schooling in the safe and proper use of plastic explosives.
Room at the Mark!	A racing hail used to indicate that there are approximately two inches between a rounding buoy and the hailee, and that the hailer intends to physically widen that distance thereby providing himself with ample "room at the mark."
Rule-of-Thumb	A formula or guide that gives a rough or practical estimate. Some rules of thumb useful in windsurfing circles are "One six-pack per person per day," "Three hot dogs per six-pack," and "One bag of nacho-cheese tortilla chips per person for the car ride."
Rust	A chemically-based decomposition caused by the gradual oxidation of ferrous metals which eventually turns all steel or iron parts on a sailboard into amorphous globs of discolored scale with the approximate structural characteristics of lime jello.

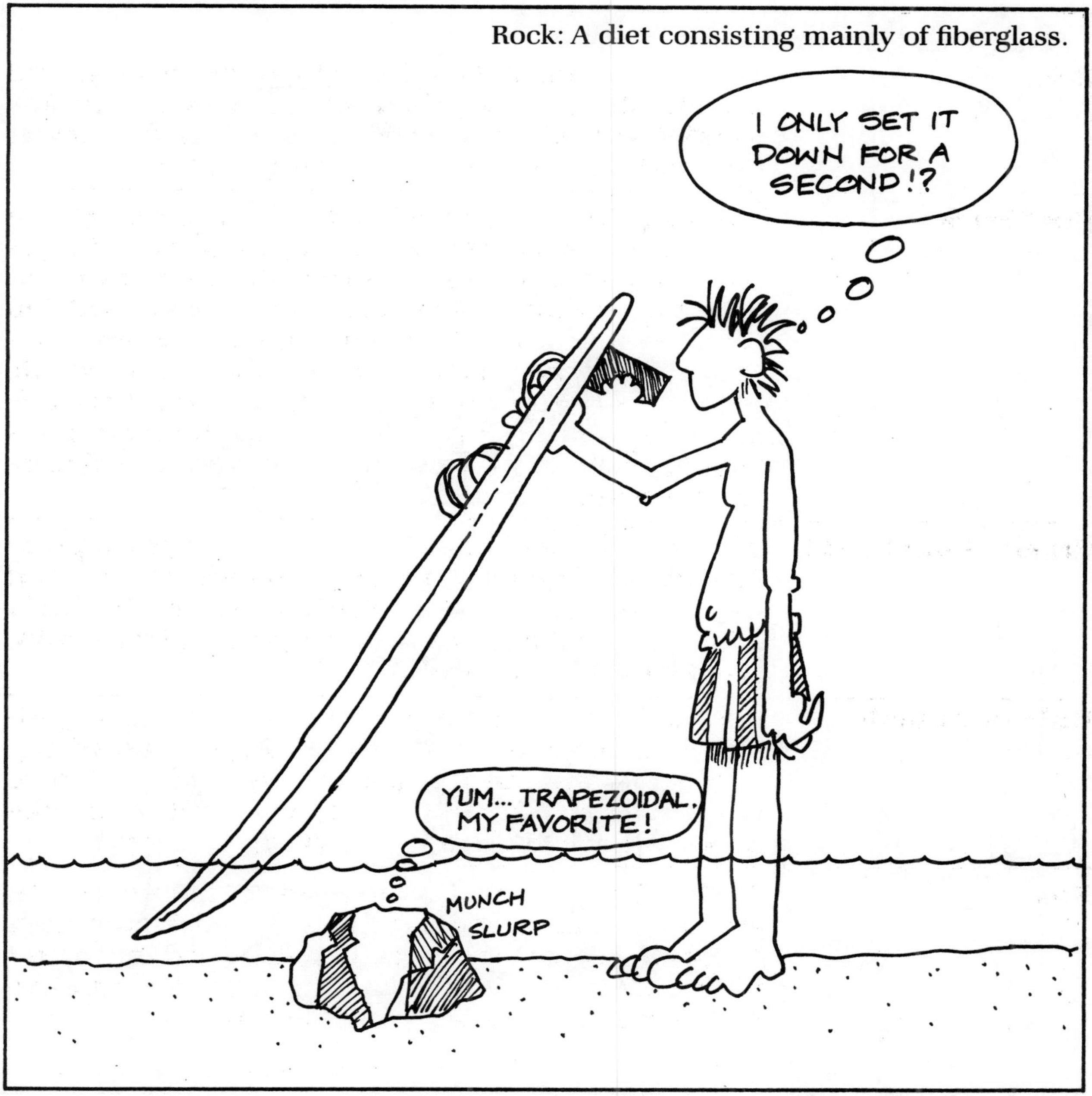

Rock: A diet consisting mainly of fiberglass.

S

Safe Quadrant

During periods of stormy or windy weather, an area of relative safety which is usually sought out by all reasonably intelligent persons and which is generally bordered by four walls, a roof and a floor and has a fireplace at one end.

Sail Window

A large, clear area of the sail intended to allow the boardsailor to see beyond the sail while sailing, thereby allowing him or her to capitalize on all potential collisions.

Salt Water

A traditional beverage of novice windsurfers.

Salutation

Method of introducing or announcing oneself. In windsurfing, some common salutations are 1) "Watch it!" 2) "Look out!!" 3) "It wasn't my fault!!!" 4) "Sorry!" 5) "Ouch!" and 6) "Oops!!"

Sand

A naturally occurring mix of fine rock aggregate and portland cement capable of instantly penetrating the deepest and most sensitive areas of a mechanism and rendering said mechanism immediately and permanently inoperable. With the possible exception of full penetration welds, sand also provides the finest method of permanently joining a mast and a mast foot.

Sandbar

The second leading cause of skeg death, surpassed only by beach starting.

Sandbar Sounding	The process by which a boardsailor determines the exact position of a sandbar by probing for it with the fin, usually at high speed. It is then customary for the boardsailor to confirm the sandbar's location by using the forehead, nose, lips or chin as a secondary probe.
Sea Room!	A nautical right-of-way hail most often used when others seem to fail.
Shark	The only thing worse than meeting Sylvester Stallone alone in a dark alley when you don't have the money you owe him.
Shi..	Phrase used by surf sailors to indicate that a wave is closing out more quickly than originally anticipated.
Shivering	The second most common action in windsurfing surpassed only by waiting.
Shorebreak	A potentially treacherous condition which occurs when waves break close to shore. During periods of large surf, getting out through the shorebreak can provide the dedicated surf sailor with a thrill and sense of accomplishment similar to that of having successfully sprinted through a live mine field. Through the years, shorebreak has been indirectly responsible for introducing the design concepts associated with such innovations as the two-piece mast, the wide-bend boom, the high-strength mast foot and the full-body cast.
Short Board	See *Sinker*.

Sandbar Sounding: An excruciatingly exact science.
HOW WILL WE EXPLAIN IT TO THE PLASTIC SURGEON THIS TIME?
AIEEE !!
SPLAT !!
LOOK MOM, DAD BROKE HIS NOSE

Sinker
Any one of various sailboard types whose physical characteristics make them impossible to sail 98% of the time.

Skeg
A specially-shaped foil installed at the tail of the board used to collect plastic bags, fast food wrappers, seaweed and other fascinating floating objects the boardsailor may want to examine more closely.

Skipper's Meeting
A ritualistic meeting of all participants in a boardsailing competition prior to the first race. The purpose of the meeting is for the referee to review the rules which govern the races. Usually these rules consist of 1) No hitting below the belt, 2) No kidney punches, 3) When I say "break," stand back, 4) I want a good clean fight, and 5) At the sound of the bell, come out swinging.

Specialty Board
A board which is custom-built to the buyer's specifications for certain wind and water conditions, namely the wind and water conditions present at the buyer's favorite sailing spot up to the day the buyer takes delivery of the board and every day after the buyer finally manages to sell the board at a four-hundred dollar loss, but not during the term of ownership except when the buyer is out of town on business.

Speed Trials
A high-cost method of assuring that the wind won't blow over two knots.

Splat
A sound made by novice boardsailors to indicate the termination of a maneuver. Often preceded by "AARGGggg!" "Yiiiii!!" or the like.

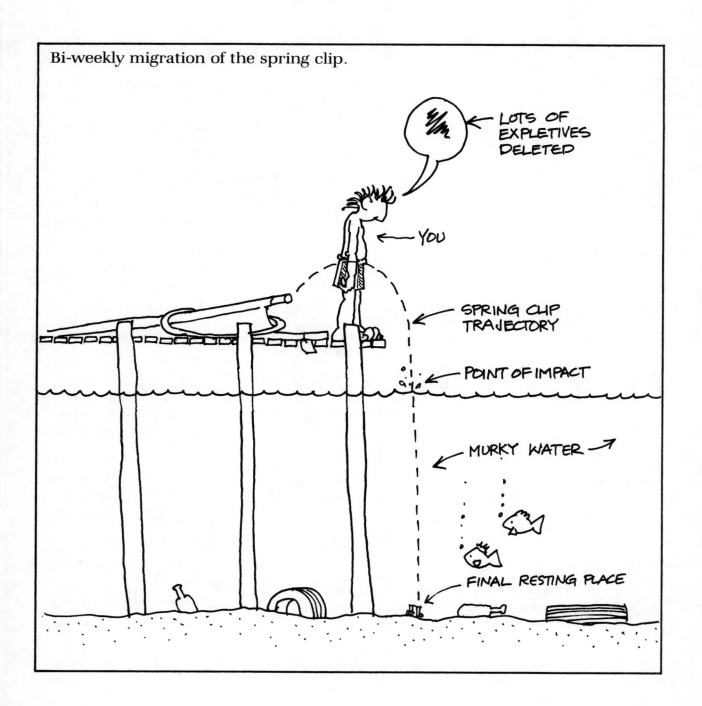

Bi-weekly migration of the spring clip.

Spring Clip	1. The essential structural bond between the board and the rig which, through some cruel twist-of-fate, has a propensity for untimely projectile flight. 2. A heavier-than-water source of frustration of astronomical proportions.
Starting Sequence	A ten-minute period preceding the start of a race during which the competitors vie for starting position limited only by the terms of the Geneva Convention.
Sucker Wind	Any wind that blows just long enough to get you to 1) Feign illness and leave work early, 2) Drive like a maniac all the way home, 3) Wreck half your gear throwing it into the car, 4) Race down to the marina and rig up, 5) Drag your board and rig down to the water, 6) Throw everything in the water, and 7) Jump aboard just as the wind totally dies so that you can sink up to your knees while you slog along at two knots struggling to stand up and muttering all those words you promised your mother you'd never repeat.
Suicide Run	As seen by sane people, any boardsailing venture which takes the boardsailor further than fifty yards from shore or into water which is greater than three feet deep.
Suntan Oil	A petroleum-based lubricant applied to the deck of a rental board by previous users.
Swell	A jolly good wave.

T

Tandem Board

A long sailboard with two complete rigs attached intended to be sailed by two people. Invented by Wolfgang Von Tandem in 1984, the tandem board enjoyed limited popularity in Germany. Unfortunately, it never really caught on in the rest of the world in part because of the periodic mysterious disappearance of the forward crew member during a day's sail. Inevitably the crew member would be found later severely bludgeoned. The mystery was solved in 1986 when an inscription at the base of the aft rig "Achung! Ist Verboten Duck Jiben!" was finally translated by a young German boardsailor visiting the United States. By then, however, the very name "tandem" was associated in consumers' minds with high fatality and all marketing ploys by the Von Tandem company to encourage use of the boards failed. Tragically, Wolfgang Von Tandem was drowned recently while testing a heavy steel plate designed to be worn by the forward crew member to prevent injury. Technical problems with the quick release buckles were cited as a major contributing factor in his untimely death.

Thingamajig

The doohickey you step on to allow the whatitz to slide forward. Thingamajigs tend to be large, hard, awkwardly positioned and, like footstraps, a major contributing factor to the medical condition known as *toejamb*.

Tandem Board: A mystery solved.

Three-sixty	An advanced and difficult windsurfing maneuver requiring great skill and courage through which the successful sailor, after much complex maneuvering, is able to sail away on the exact same heading as before beginning the maneuver, only going much slower. This maneuver is also known as the "useless loop," the "senseless circle," and the "pointless pirouette."
Tonnage Rule	The nautical right-of-way rule which states that, all other rules not withstanding, the biggest boat has the right-of-way. Since a sailboard weighs forty pounds or so, about 1/50,000th the weight of the next largest boat in existence, this is a good rule for boardsailors to know, especially when encountering freighters, frigates, aircraft carriers and the like.
Triathlon	A three-part athletic competition used by boardsailors to hone the skills most vital to their sport. Part One of the competition tests the participant's abilities to withdraw a sail from a car-mounted roof rack without first removing the fourteen other items of windsurfing paraphernalia piled on top. Part Two tests the participant's abilities to drink large quantities of beer while simultaneously complaining about the lack of wind. And Part Three tests the participant's abilities to explain to a spouse or mate how it's possible to spend the whole day windsurfing if there was never any wind. Although not yet Olympic in stature, the Boardsailing Triathlon is rapidly becoming one of the most popular athletic events with thousands of boardsailors training arduously and thoroughly every weekend.

Tonnage Rule: Vessels listed in decreasing right-of-way order.

#1: FREIGHTERS

2: BARGES

#3 LARGE PLEASURE CRAFT

#4 SMALLER PLEASURE CRAFT

#5: INNER TUBES, RAFTS, FLOTSAM & GNATS

#6: JETSAM AND WINDSURFERS

Trunk: The seasonal cleaning thereof (gearbag similar).

Trunk	An automobile storage area used by boardsailors to store wet gear and develop new strains of rust and mold.

U

Universal	The flexible joint between the sailboard and the mast which revolutionized sailing by creating the vessel which is now known generically as the *windsurfer* and enabling the maneuver which is now known generically as the *face plant*.
Unloading	A process by which the boardsailor extracts, usually with great force and sometimes resulting in extensive property damage or personal injury, the piece of gear lowest on the roof racks or most deeply buried in the car trunk, without first removing any of the other gear.
Upgrade	The process of selling off your perfectly good old gear at 25 percent of its value in order to buy all new gear, driven mainly by the fear that one of your friends might buy new gear and become faster than you.
Uphauling	1. A windsurfing maneuver through which the novice boardsailor is introduced to the nautical principle of the sea anchor. 2. The worst part about learning to windsurf.

Waiting: The importance of owning the escape vehicle.

V

Van

A large, fully-enclosed cargo vehicle used by windsurfers as a depository for cracked masts, bent booms, broken fins, empty beer cans, beach sand, junk-food wrappers and other natural by-products of their sport.

Variable

Anything on a sailboard that isn't permanently fixed in position by salt, sand, mud, rust, corrosion, deformation or any combination thereof.

W

Waiting

1. An ancient and arduous ritual performed by boardsailors on the beach during periods of little or no wind. This ritual is generally marked by excessive consumption of beer and the nearly constant use of phrases like, "I think it's coming up!" 2. An equally ancient, albeit vastly more arduous, ritual performed on the beach by non-boardsailing spouses and mates during periods of moderate or heavy wind. This ritual is generally marked by the excessive consumption of hot chocolate or similar beverages and the almost constant use of phrases like, "Maybe this *is* grounds for divorce!"

Waterstart	A freestyle maneuver through which the boardsailor changes positions from face-up in the water on the windward-side of the board to face-down in the water on the leeward-side of the board.
Wave Sailor	A cross between Godzilla and a kamikaze pilot whose primary avocation is buying new windsurfing gear to replace the demolished stuff.
Waves	Large, moving bodies of water which roam the oceans in sets seeking out windsurfing equipment on which to feed.
Weather Forecasting	A form of medieval witchcraft through which practitioners, by dressing in outlandish costumes and waving strange wands and cords, believe they can predict the future. Today, although tolerated, weather forecasting is generally seen as quackery.
Weather Radio	A small transistor-type radio which is usually found in every avid boardsailor's glove compartment under four maps and a six-month-old bag of half-eaten french fries and whose primary use is for storing dead, nine-volt batteries.
Wetsuit Zipper	Any one of a class of zippers prone to instantaneous corrosion when used in the presence of water.
Whale	A large, ocean-going mammal rarely encountered by boardsailors; the observation of which is considered to be an indication that: 1) It's lost, or 2) You're really lost.
Whitecap	An omen, often occurring in large numbers, seen by boardsailors as an indication of that elusive climatic quantity called "wind." The appearance of one

Waterstart: An alternate method of swimming.

STEP #1

STEP #2

SPLASH!

STEP #3

Wind Direction: Determination thereof.

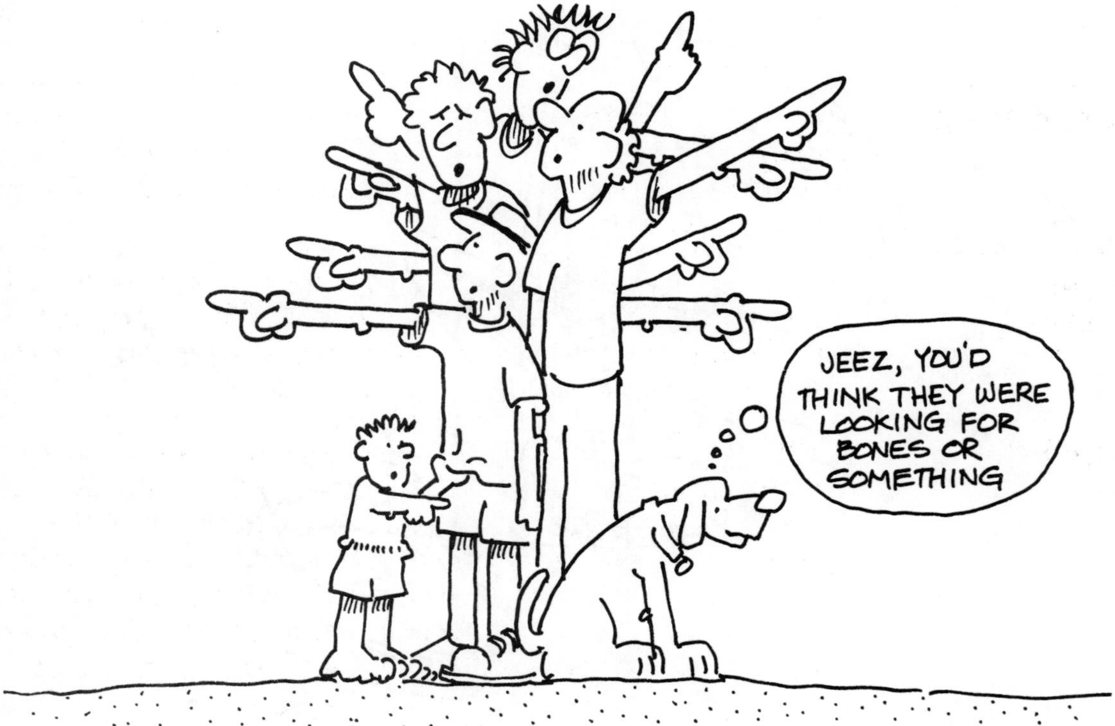

whitecap is usually sufficient to prompt a riot-like beachside rigging session known as a *rigging frenzy*.

Wind	A climatically-driven movement of air essential to the sport of windsurfing the presence of which, through some cruel twist-of-fate, is usually restricted to weekdays between the hours of 9:00 am and 5:00 pm.
Wind Direction	One of several physical qualities of wind the knowledge of which, although impossible to pinpoint, is absolutely essential to every beginning windsurfing maneuver.
Windsearching	A ritualistic quest, equaled in the annals of history only by that for the Holy Grail, performed every weekend afternoon by tens-of-thousands of boardsailors worldwide.
Windspeed, Apparent	The wind's velocity as it appears to an observer. This can differ from the *true windspeed* for many reasons; the most notable of which are fear, panic and the concern for one's life.
Windspeed, True	The wind's velocity as it is measured at a stationary point with objective scientific instruments. It is common knowledge among boardsailors, however, that these scientific instruments rarely function properly and almost always underreport the actual windspeed. For that reason the *apparent windspeed* is generally accepted as a much more accurate account of actual wind conditions.
Windsurfing Etiquette	To insure that all newcomers to the sport of windsurfing are welcomed equally, the windsurfing community has set up some informal rules of etiquette. While there are plenty of variations, generally speak-

ing each time a boardsailor goes sailing he or she will attempt to 1) Seek out a beginning boardsailor who is having difficulties, 2) Wait until that boardsailor finally gets their sail uphauled and begins sailing, 3) Sail just to windward of them blocking their wind and causing them to fall, 4) Continually use them as a jibing buoy as they attempt to uphaul, 5) Watch as they hopelessly drift downwind to the mud flats, 6) Laugh as they drag all their gear over the rocks to get to the service road, and 7) Casually drink beer and snicker as they slog back into the rigging area forty-five minutes later. Of course, a completely different set of etiquette rules apply if the beginner is a cute blond of the opposite sex.

Wipeout	An abrupt and generally undesired termination of a windsurfing maneuver, the execution of which tends to diminish both the boardsailor's confidence and good-looks.
World Speed Record	A championship mark held by Edward "Fast Eddie" Friedman of Greensboro, North Carolina who on May 7th, 1981, successfully derigged his sail, changed from his wetsuit to his street clothes, loaded his gear atop his car, found the nearest bar and ordered a beer, all in 2 minutes and 47 seconds. Being true competitors at heart, most boardsailors practice this type of speed competition every afternoon in hopes that one day they will be able to challenge Fast Eddie's time.
Wrist Rotation	One of the most repeated of all windsurfing motions. To practice, hold your wallet in your left hand, reach into the wallet with your right hand and grasp the three largest bills available ($20.00 minimum) be-

tween your thumb and your forefinger. Then flick your wrist releasing your grasp at precisely the right time to allow the bills to wantonly float to a countertop or similar surface while repeating the popular incantation, "Give me one of those, too." The whole trick to this maneuver is never to attempt to sum the bills as they leave your wallet as this could lead to acute depression. Simply keep repeating the procedure until you run out of bills or someone tells you to stop.

Z

Zero Degrees Kelvin

The temperature at which all molecular motion ceases, which is equivalent to -459.6 degrees Fahrenheit. Ten degrees Kelvin is the temperature at which most avid windsurfers believe it's warm enough to go sailing, unless of course, they own a drysuit.

Zoom Lens

High-powered camera lens with which your friends and relatives can photographically capture every mistake you make.

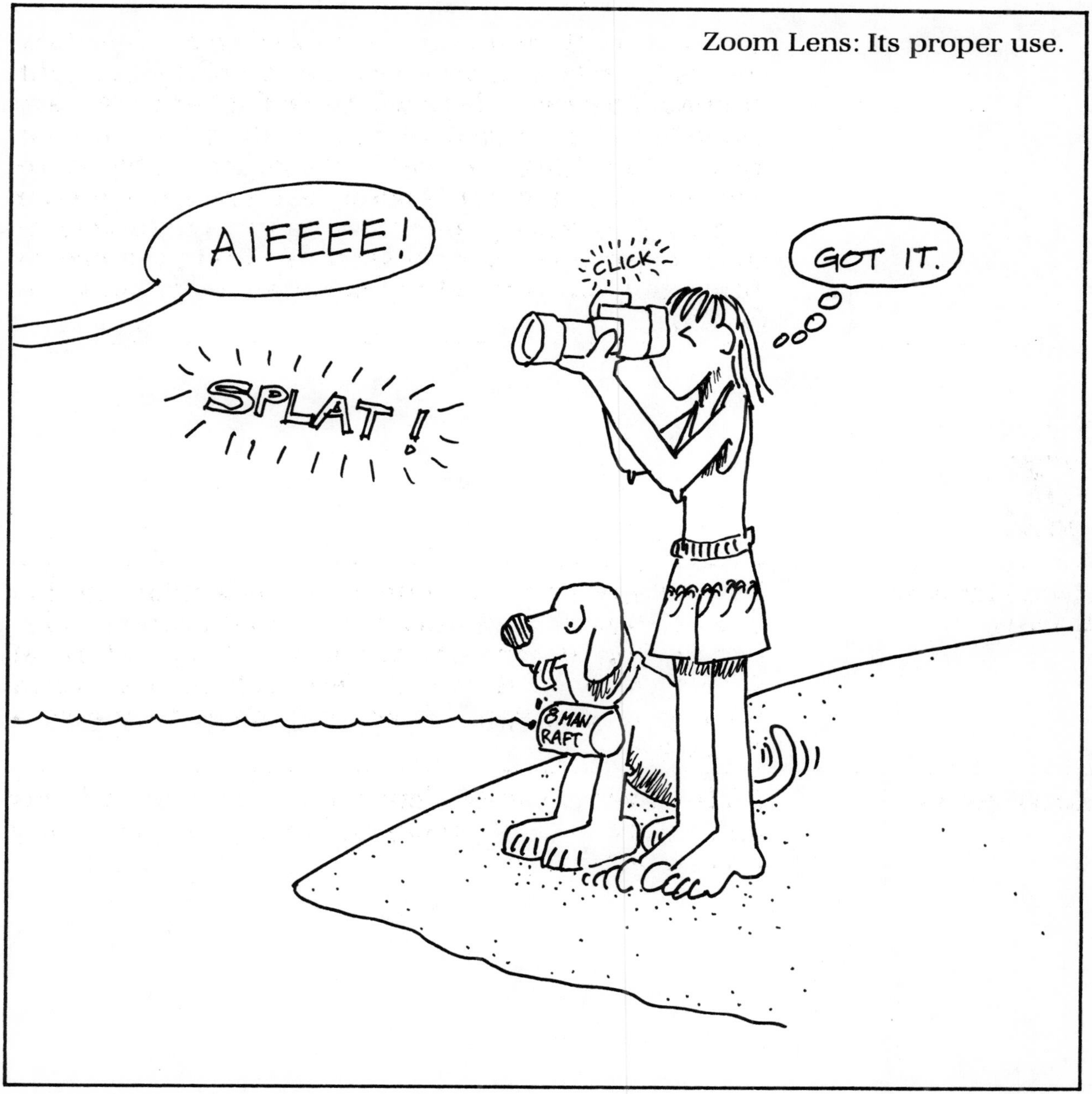

Zoom Lens: Its proper use.